The B·I·B·L·E is for me!

Written by Tami Myers Sleeper

Illustrated by Emily Zieroth

WestBow Press books may be ordered through booksellers or by contacting:

WestBow Press
A Division of Thomas Nelson & Zondervan
1663 Liberty Drive
Bloomington, IN 47403
www.westbowpress.com
1 (866) 928-1240

Interior Image Credit: Emily Zieroth

ISBN: 978-1-9736-9459-5 (sc)
ISBN: 978-1-9736-9460-1 (e)

Library of Congress Control Number: 2020911536

Print information available on the last page.

WestBow Press rev. date: 07/31/2020

WestBow
PRESS®
A DIVISION OF THOMAS NELSON
& ZONDERVAN

For my Lockly

Be Brave ♥ Have Faith ♥ Smile

ilyatinycdai

With Genesis, you start the Bible to begin
Out with a bang Revelation will be the end.

The Bible is pretty long with 66 books in all
Reading all those names in a trance, you may fall

But don't give up hope if you get
confused or start to tire
Because with this good book you
will avoid that great fire.

Learn about God, and he will give you his grace
And with his love, you will win this very long race.

Within seven days, only one very short week
God made everything, from the big sky to every small creek.

Heaven and Earth were the first for God to make
This started the process, which was good for all our sake.

On day two came the sky, and don't ask me
why, but it's as blue as blue can be,
almost as blue as the sea, which by the way came on day three.

Next came the full moon and very bright sun
So we know when to go to bed and when to have fun.

All those fishes and birds came on day five
I know the birds sang and were happy to be alive.

On the sixth day, God gave us all the animals and man
Which he wants us to love and take care of as best we can.

On day seven God decided everything was
good, so he then took a rest
For he had created everything on Earth and given us his very best.

In the garden, the first man Adam was with his wife Eve
God told them one tree was bad, but they didnt believe.

The fruit from the tree Adam and Eve both ate
God saw this, and they were in for a sad fate.

Adam then had to work hard to get food from the field
And it was difficult for Eve a family to build

But God stayed close to them, right by their side
Because his great love for them he just could not hide.

Noah knew it would start raining
So he started doing some praying.

After lots of hard work he built an ark, a big boat
He used it to save his family and all
the animals, even the goat.

When the rain came after many days and nights
He released a bird to fly around and see the sights.

After more floating, the bird never came back around
and Noah figured he must have found dry ground.

This was a sign from God to Noah that
the waters were going down
Pretty soon they would be able to
leave the boat and not drown.

God then made a promise with a rainbow in the sky
To never again flood the Earth, and in that, we can rely.

A long, long time ago, God's people were enslaved
God felt bad and gave them freedom if only they behaved.

He promised to lead them to a beautiful new land
But they had to go through the desert, the sun, and the sand.

They even had to cross a river that was running very strong
But God separated the waters so they could simply walk along.

Finally, after wondering the desert for 40 hard years
God showed them their home, and they had no more fears.

They were rewarded because in God they believed
They trusted in him and this beautiful land they received.

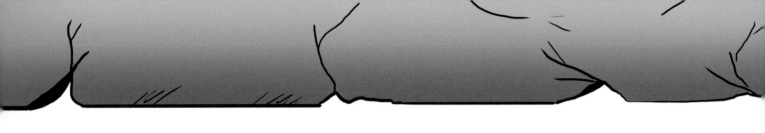

God gave Moses 10 commandments to give to His people
Moses was up on a mountain, not in a church under a steeple.

Rule #1 and 2 go together, and he started with the most important of all, love God and nothing more!
Rule #3 says not to curse and speak God's name in anger because your mouth is a window to your core.

#4 says we need to rest and focus on God one day a week
Onto #5, telling us to love your Mom and Dad and their approval you should seek.

#6 commands to not hurt or hate anyone
just because you might be mad
#7 goes on to say be faithful to your spouse,
and if not, God will be sad.

Rule #8 declares you should not take what
is not yours, you should not steal
And #9 says to always be honest and tell
the truth, no matter how you feel.

Finally, in #10, God wants us to be happy with what he has given us.
And just because someone may have more, we shouldn't make a fuss.

Samson was a man of God and was really big and strong
His girlfriend Delilah was mean and did something very wrong.

God gave Samson his strength through his long hair
But Delilah was greedy, and for him she didn't care.

While he was sleeping, she cut it all off, shaved his head
With no strength left he could barely get out of bed.

His enemies came and took him away
They made him blind, and in prison, he had to stay.

But God was with him when his hair started to grow back
And he was able to defeat his foes with a one-man attack.

Ruth was a great friend as her name implies
She was more loyal than anyone could realize.

Ruth, to her mother in law, was her best friend
She stayed with her even though her
marriage had come to an end.

Their husbands, without leaving
very much had died.
So they went back home together
with no one by their side.

Ruth worked very hard and to a
good man finally got married
But together the women stayed until
in the ground they were buried.

David and Goliath is a story that has many times been told.
Goliath was a huge giant and David
was just a boy but very bold.

An angry man was Goliath who was
mean and liked to fight
But David was brave and stood up to him
because he had God in his sight.

He approached the giant with only a slingshot and a stone
It only took one try, he hit the giant, and
he fell dead without even a groan.

The story spread about David, and he
was famous all over the land
He eventually became a King just like
God had already planned.

David had a son named Solomon when he was King
When he got old and was dying, he chose
Solomon to the throne to bring.

God loved Solomon and asked him
what he wanted in life
He was surprised by his answer, not
power, money or even a wife.

Solomon asked only for knowledge and to be smart
God was happy with his answer, it touched his heart.

God gave him the knowledge to be
smarter than any other man
He used his wisdom to rule the people
and a great country he ran.

Because he was a good man, God also
gave him the money and power
And he continued to rule God's
people until his last hour.

Job was a good man who gave God all his trust
The Devil didn't like him so into a
sad game he was thrust.

The Devil said if he lost everything, he would
turn from God, and his faith would be lost
God allowed the Devil to take his kids,
animals and wealth, but Job's faith
didn't falter no matter the cost.

Then the Devil took his health, but
he wasn't allowed to kill
But Job withstood him because he
knew God's love was real.

Because of Job's strong faith, trust and love
God gave him his life back with
blessings from above.

Proverbs is a book we can
look to for advice
It is not hard to read but
it is simple and concise.

Even though it was written a long time ago,
God gave the wisdom to us to bestow.

The advice will always be good and true
And applies to everyone, not just a few.

Listen close to the words
and try to live right
By staying on the right path
with God in your sight.

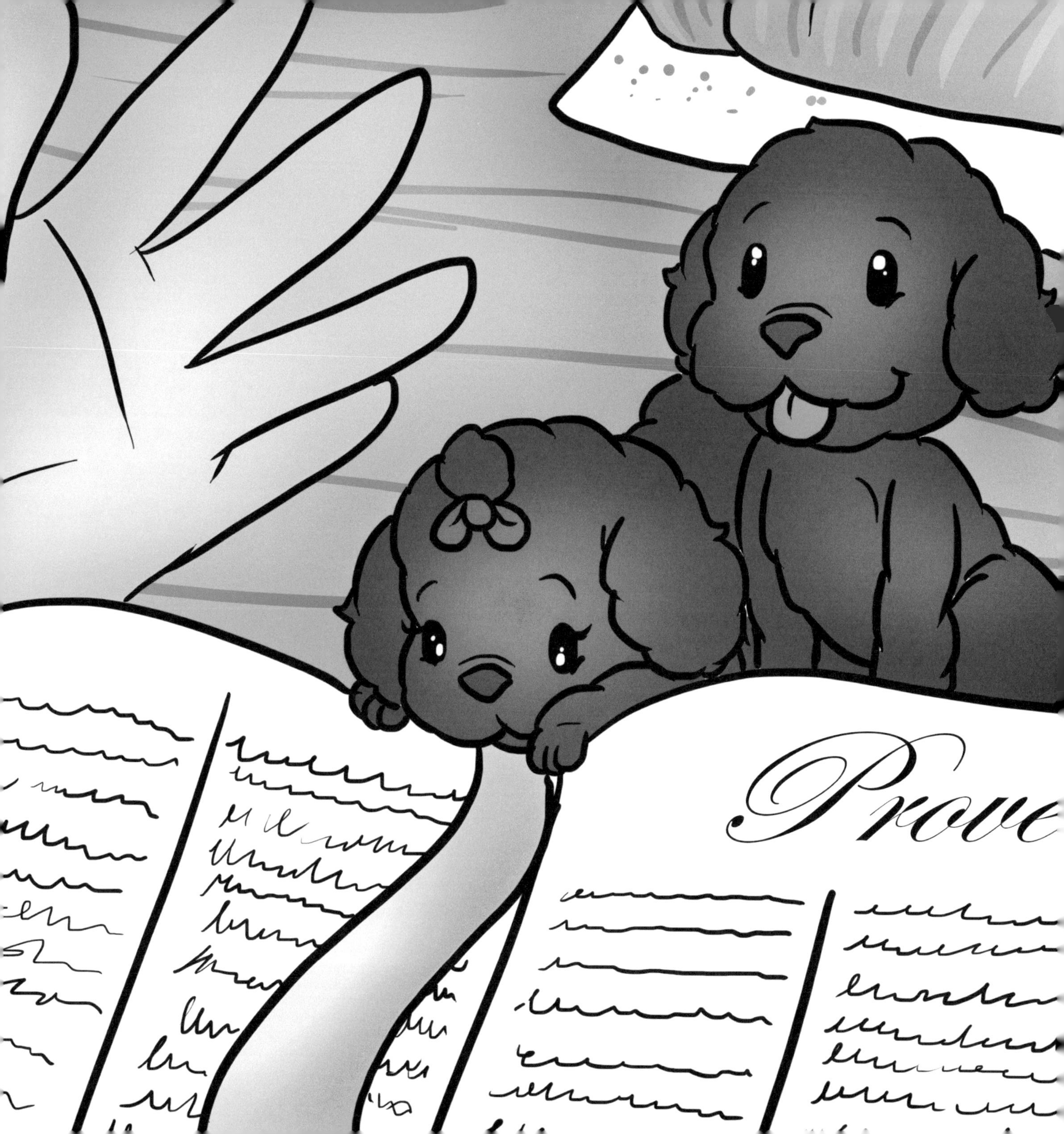
Prove

Shadrach, Meshach and Abednego
worshiped God and no other idols,
The King didn't like that, so he wanted
to kill them without even trials.

He ordered them to be tied up and thrown
into a furnace, by fire to die
They were content because they knew God would
protect them and send a strong reply.

After the King saw four men in the fire, the story did turn
He called them to come out, each did, without even a burn.

The King then changed his mind and said God was good
God had protected his sons just as they knew he would.

The Lord told Jonah to go to a scary place to preach his word
Jonah was afraid and pretended the command he had not heard.

He tried to run away and hide, onto a boat to set sail
God could still see him that's when be brought in a whale.

A bad storm came in one night, the men didn't know what to do
Jonah said, 'it's my fault, throw me overboard,' and so he flew.

The huge whale came and swallowed him whole
God kept him alive in order to cleanse his soul.

After the number of days and nights hit three
The whale swam to shore to set Jonah free.

Jonah then did as God had said, for fear he didn't care
Plus he ended up with an amazing story for us all to share.

Jesus was born to a young woman named Mary
She wasn't yet married, so his
birth was quite contrary.

God brought Jesus down to Earth
to be like you and me
So we didn't have to follow so many
rules, and we could live free.

He wasn't born a rich man, well known or in power
But he changed the world from his
first breath to his last hour.

Jesus taught the people that
God, his father was good
And all we had to do was be like
him as much as we could.

At first, people loved Jesus because
their illnesses he did cure
But soon some people got mad, and they
weren't nice that's for sure.

They were jealous and plotted against
him, making an evil plan
They treated him like a criminal even
though he was a perfect man.

The mobs put him on a cross to make him suffer and die
After six hours, Jesus gave up and cried, 'Father, why?'.

Jesus died hanging on a cross, but that's
not the end of the story, not quite
They buried him in a cave, but in three
days he arose with his own might.

He came back to life, he was no longer dead
He awoke and walked with his friends just as he had said.

Jesus then went to Heaven to live with God forever
But his tie with his people he did not sever.

When he left, to each of his children
he had a gift to give
He sent the Holy Spirit from Heaven
into each believer to live.

When you do something wrong, that's
the voice inside your head
It keeps us on the right path and
helps us live like God instead.

It will make us happy in life if only
we pay attention and hear
If we follow its guidance, we will
live forever, without fear.

Paul was a man who hated Jesus and
wasn't good, not good at all
His goal was to punish and kill those that
believed in Jesus and see them fall.

One day God met him along a road and told him
to change his ways because he was wrong
Instead, he needed to believe in Jesus and teach
people about him and be brave and strong.

To convince him, for three days, God closed
his eyes, made him unable to see
After the three days, God opened his eyes
so his faith to others he could decree.

He changed his ways and started
to teach like God had said
Paul gave up his life and traveled and
preached wherever God led.

Many people began to believe in Jesus because of Paul
All because he listened when God made his call.

The New Testament has several
letters that Paul wrote
Many written to churches that
Paul could brag on and dote.

He gave them encouragement
to keep their faith true
He told them he loved them
and that God did too.

Paul asked them for prayers and
said some for them as well
He prayed they would stay strong and
not believe lies others might tell.

For people and God, Paul had
a lot of love to give
He wanted peace, happiness, and
a life for all with God to live.

Revelation comes and brings the Bible to an end
It can be very scary, but only
for those that have sinned.

There are lots of monsters and weird
things that make it hard to understand
But we don't have to worry because God
loves us and he will always be in command.

The bad stuff will happen to
those that don't believe
So always be prepared and by
God's side never leave.

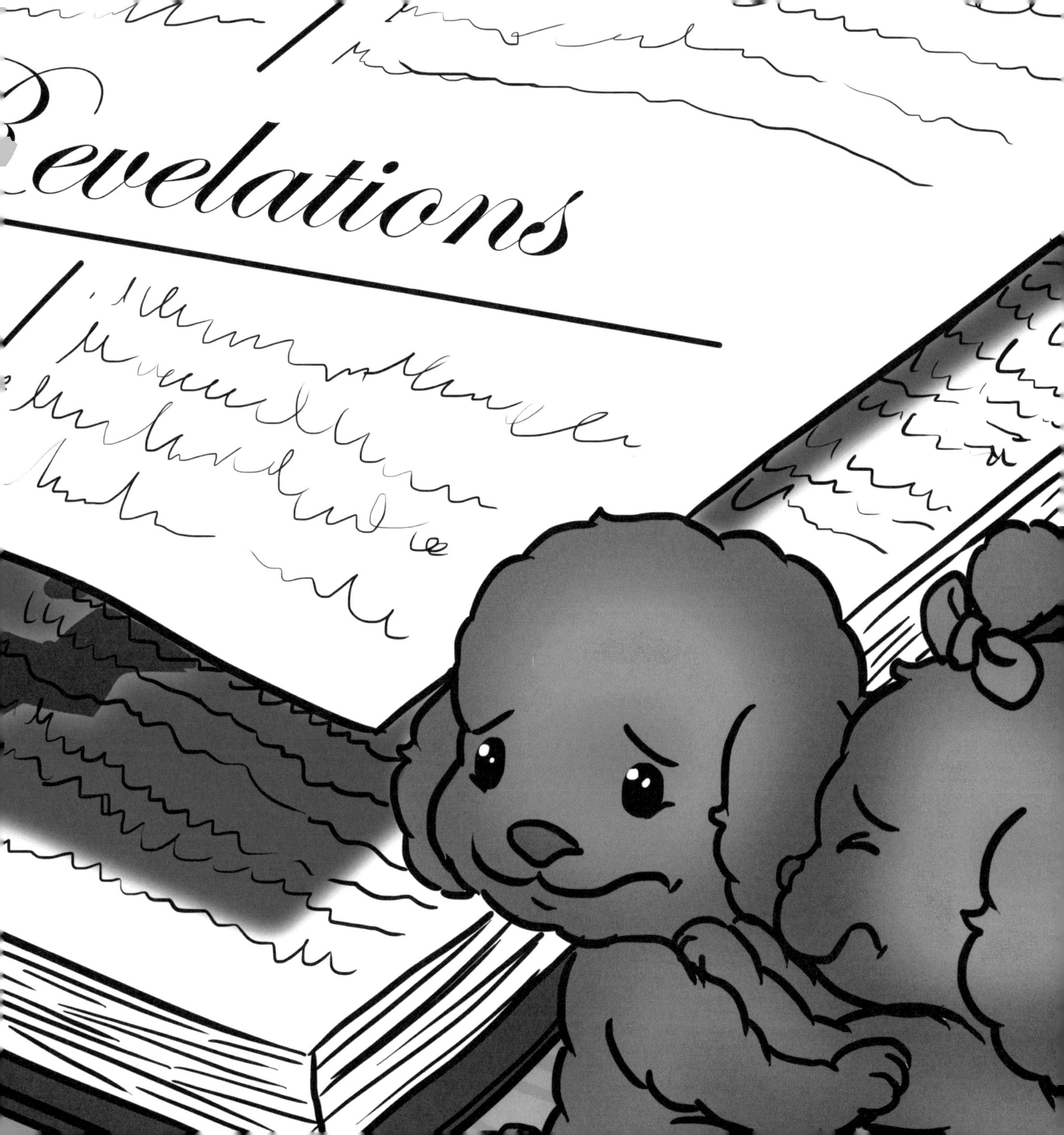
Revelations

With that the Bible is complete
If you read it all, you accomplished quite a feat.

Although you may not understand
everything you read
Just know that God always told the
truth in each word he said.

Always remember in good times and bad,
That God loves you more than
anything he's ever had.

Have faith in God and in Heaven
a perfect home he will give
And you will be right by his side forever to live.

Amen.

Old Testament

Genesis	Proverbs	Malachi
Exodus	Ecclesiastes	
Leviticus	Song of Songs	
Numbers	Isaiah	
Deuteronomy	Jeremiah	
Joshua	Lamentations	
Judges	Ezekiel	
Ruth	Daniel	
1 Samuel	Hosea	
2 Samuel	Joel	
1 Kings	Amos	
2 Kings	Obadiah	
1 Chronicles	Jonah	
2 Chronicles	Micah	
Ezra	Nahum	
Nehemiah	Habakkuk	
Esther	Zephaniah	
Job	Haggai	
Psalms	Zechariah	

New Testament

Matthew	James
Mark	1 Peter
Luke	2 Peter
John	1 John
Acts	2 John
Romans	3 John
1 Corinthians	Jude
2 Corinthians	Revelation
Galatians	
Ephesians	
Philippians	
Colossians	
1 Thessalonians	
2 Thessalonians	
1 Timothy	
2 Timothy	
Titus	
Philemon	
Hebrews	

About the Author

Tami is a wife and mother of one young son, Lock, and two poodles which she adores, 410 and Yogi. Her desire to strengthen the faith of her son along with her creativity and not to forget her passion for poodles, motivated her to create this book based on the Bible. Tami has never shied away from a challenge and has always taken advantage of any opportunity to expand her horizons and experience a life with no regrets. From sky diving to being an inducted member of the National Skeet Shooters Hall of Fame, if she sees an opportunity to live a fuller life, she takes it and devotes 100% to the task at hand. Similarly, she pours her heart and soul into this book with the vision of making the Bible more understandable, accessible and personal for anyone that this book touches.

Printed in the United States
By Bookmasters